What Can We Take Away from the Renaissance Period?

History Book for Kids 9-12
Children's Renaissance Books

BABY PROFESSOR
EDUCATION KIDS

Speedy Publishing LLC

40 E. Main St. #1156

Newark, DE 19711

www.speedypublishing.com

Copyright 2017

In this book, we're going to talk about the influence that the Renaissance period has had on our modern world. So, let's get right to it!

WHAT WAS THE RENAISSANCE?

Between 1300 AD through 1700 AD, there was a complete transformation of culture and art in Europe. This period is called the Renaissance and the word "Renaissance" means "rebirth." This rebirth began in Italy and then spread through the surrounding countries of Europe.

MIDDLE AGES CASTLE

At this time, Italy didn't have one central government. Instead, they had powerful city-states that were frequently at war with each other. Despite this political instability, culture once again began to flourish after the many dark centuries of the Middle Ages.

THE MIDDLE AGES

In 476 AD the Roman Empire fell. It had been the dominant force in Europe for over 1,000 years. This is the event that marked the beginning of the Middle Ages. Advances in the arts and sciences as well as in the principles of government that had been created by the ancient Greeks and the Romans began to disappear.

ROMAN LIGHTHOUSE

It was almost as if someone had a library filled with all the knowledge in the world and then the lights were turned out. No one had access to the knowledge anymore or even remembered it. This is, in a sense, what

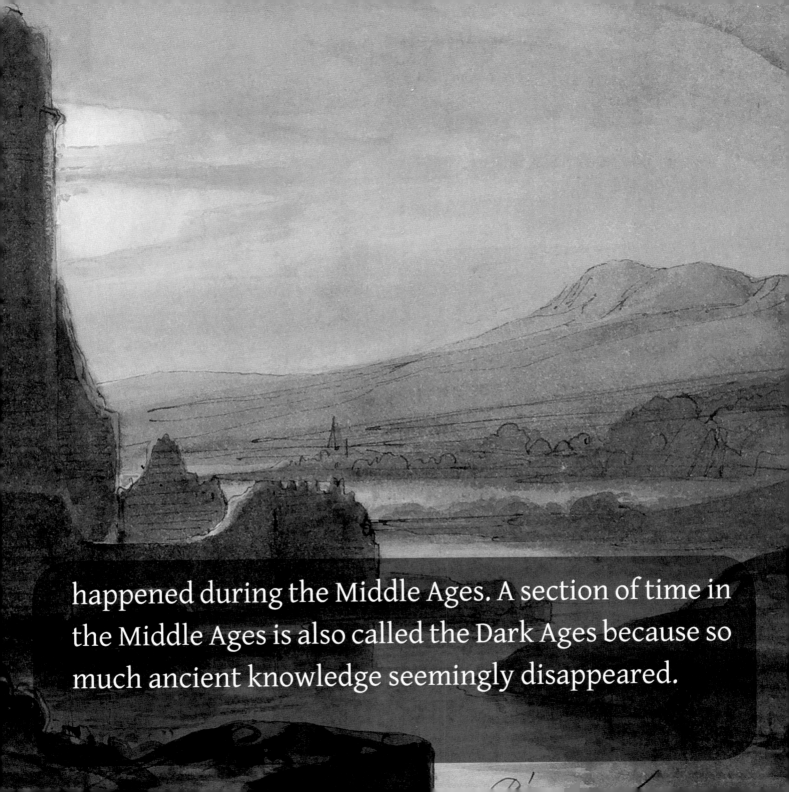

happened during the Middle Ages. A section of time in the Middle Ages is also called the Dark Ages because so much ancient knowledge seemingly disappeared.

None of these changes happened overnight. It was a very gradual process. The culture digressed from a thriving arts-oriented society to one where its citizens had lives of endless suffering and pain. Another practice that had been a common one among the ancient Roman population had been the art of bathing for cleanliness.

ROMAN BATH

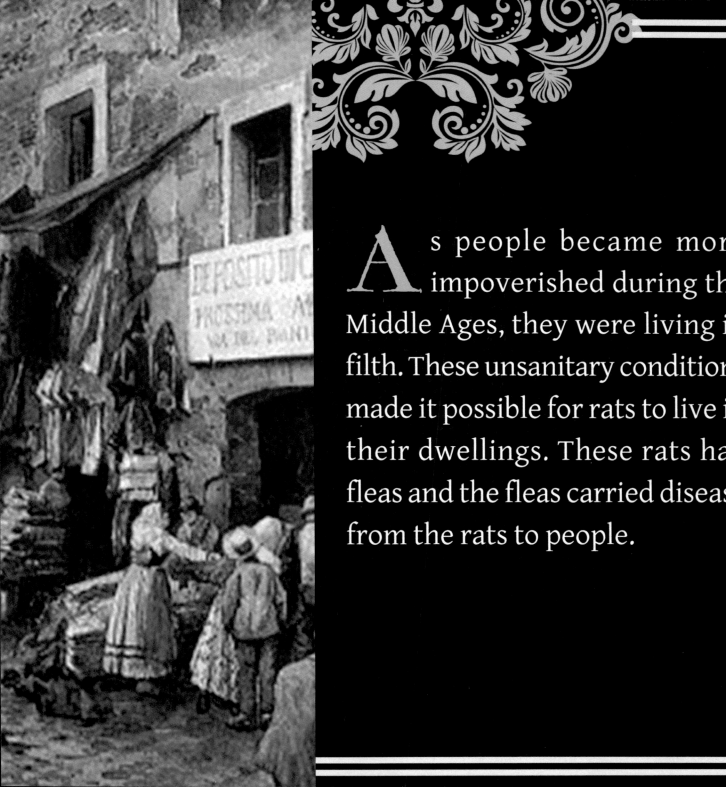

As people became mor[e] impoverished during th[e] Middle Ages, they were living i[n] filth. These unsanitary condition[s] made it possible for rats to live i[n] their dwellings. These rats ha[d] fleas and the fleas carried disea[se] from the rats to people.

This was the start of the Black Death, a form of bubonic plague, which eventually wiped out a third of the entire population of Europe. This horrendous day-to-day existence revolving around starvation, sickness, and death, was ingrained into the people's hearts and minds. They just couldn't envision a better future.

Black Death

They had kept true to their religion and obeyed the Catholic Church and yet they had received suffering and death. Many of them believed that God had punished them by bringing the Black Death to their cities and towns. They didn't realize that their own unsanitary practices had brought the dreaded disease to them.

Catholic Church

Black Death

THE START OF A NEW ERA

At the beginning of the 14th century, Italy was ready for a transformation. Between 1346 and 1353, the Black Death had wiped out so many people that it changed the way the economy was working. With fewer people ready and willing to work, those who survived were making better wages. Because there were less people, there was more wealth and more resources to go around.

When wages are good, people's attitudes change quickly. They are no longer on the edge of starvation and they can afford to buy the food they need to survive. As their situation improves, they can also afford to buy luxury items and enjoy creature comforts.

WHAT WAS HUMANISM?

As Florence, one of Italy's powerful city-states, became wealthier during the period of the late 1300s and the 1400s, the people began to start thinking differently about what life meant and how their lives could be changed for the better.

Scholars, philosophers, and writers began to study the ancient civilizations that had existed before the Middle Ages. They found a tremendous amount of inspiration in these ancient cultures. They didn't necessarily want to abandon religion. Instead, they just wanted their lives to turn away from the doom and gloom aspect of religion.

FLORENCE

SARDINIA CHURCH, MIDDLE AGES

They realized that these ancient cultures had flourishing art, architecture, philosophy, literature, poetry, and science. They wanted to revive these wonderful aspects of culture so they could live a better life and give a better life to their children.

This change in thinking resulted in the principles of Humanism. Humanism was a philosophy that allowed people to feel good about bringing comfort and culture into their lives. This philosophy turned away from the medieval scholasticism, which had focused almost exclusively on the dogma and tradition of the Catholic Church. Instead, religion was only one of the components of a rich inner life.

PALACE OF CAPRAROLA

Breathtaking art, harmonious music, beautiful architecture, and a comfortable place to live filled with objects that provided comfort were things that were seen as important to life once again. The principles of Humanism drove people to strive for the best in all the experiences that life has to offer and to pursue opportunities to become educated and cultured. Art became more expressive as the realism and emotion of the human experience was depicted.

WHY WAS THE RENAISSANCE IMPORTANT?

Throughout human history there have been times when not much innovation or new thinking occurs and then there have been other times when it seems like explosions are happening in every industry, in the arts, and in science.

The Renaissance was vitally important because it was a golden age for human development just as the ancient Greek and Roman civilizations had been in their day. This is why the people of the Renaissance turned to these two ancient civilizations for their inspiration. Inspiration spreads fast. These changing ideas were like new wellsprings of crystal clear water that started to flow all over Europe as local thinking and cultures blended with the principles set out in Humanism.

What followed was a boom in exploration and trade around the world. After all, it was during the Renaissance that Italian explorer Christopher Columbus claimed the New World for Spain. Exploration expeditions and even military campaigns were started with a greater zest since a victorious army could bring with it a new stronger government and a faster cultural change.

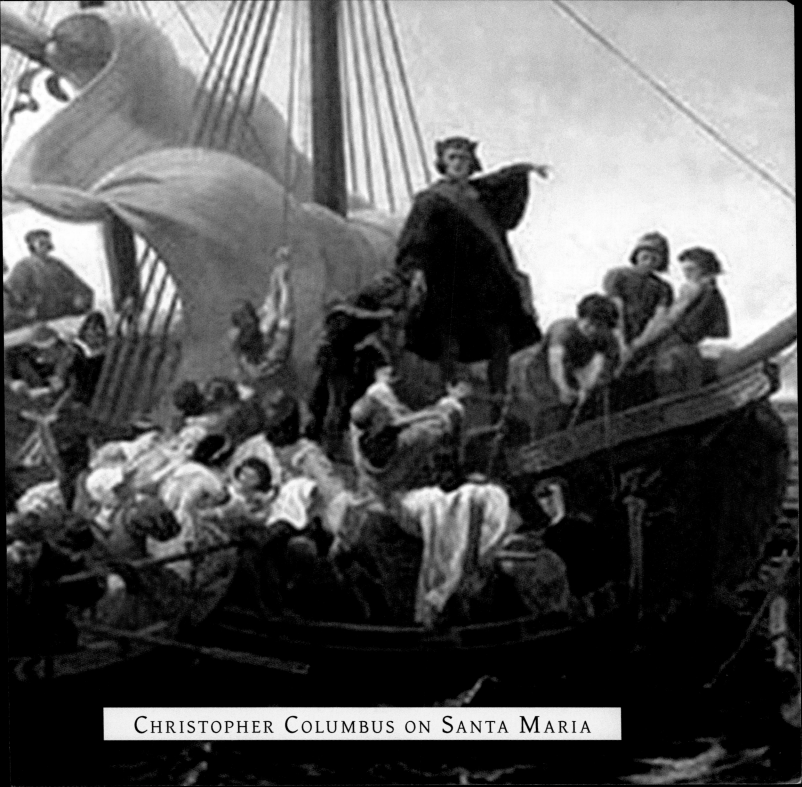

CHRISTOPHER COLUMBUS ON SANTA MARIA

NATIVITAS TVA DEI GENITRIX VIRGO GAVDIVM ANNVNTIAVIT VNIVERSO MVNDO

St. Anne in a Renaissance room

The Renaissance completely changed the way people viewed the world. It also had a cumulative effect, like a snowball that gathers snow as it rolls down a hill. Every new advancement led to new discoveries and innovations.

THE MEDICI FAMILY, PATRONS OF THE ARTS

At the pinnacle of Italian society there were new groups of rulers. These rulers, like the Medici family of Florence, were patrons of art and culture and admired the ancient civilizations of the Greeks and Romans. They aspired to that greatness themselves.

MEDICI FAMILY AS SAINTS

ALESSANDRO DE' MEDICI, RULER OF FLORENCE

The Medici family began as bankers and as their wealth grew so did their influence. They supported the Humanist movement and were excellent at recognizing talent in the artists who approached them for commissions. Eventually, they became the rulers of Florence's city-state and wielded even more power.

As the classics from antiquity came back to the forefront, masterful artists such as Leonardo da Vinci, Raphael, and Botticelli took the mythology, heroes, and stories and wove them into their work with a more modern approach. Michelangelo recast stories from the Old Testament into modern mythologies that resembled these ancient works.

MICHELANGELO BUONARROTI

IONAS

LAST JUDGEMENT

In Michelangelo's painting, the Last Judgement, over the Sistine Chapel altar, Christ is painted almost as if he were Hercules from Greek and Roman mythology. This dynamic Christ is as strong and as powerful as an athlete as he casts those who are not worthy into hell.

The art of the Renaissance wasn't content with idealism. There was a new understanding of human anatomy underlying every sculpture and every painting. Both Leonardo and Michelangelo did studies of the human anatomy that would rival any medical artist's work today. New understanding of how to develop perspective in a drawing with light and shadow was bringing more depth to paintings and sculptures. Humans and their beautiful world were being represented with a realism that hadn't been seen before.

LEONARDO DA VINCI

Galileo Galilei

HOW DID THE RENAISSANCE IMPACT SCIENCE?

Although the Catholic Church was still fighting innovations in science, Galileo used a telescope he had made himself to study the surface of the moon. He developed a deep understanding of the celestial bodies in our solar system and beyond.

COPERNICUS

e agreed with the theories that Copernic
stated centuries before—the sun was the
olar system, not the Earth. Thanks to his c
nd his position and the courage of others, s
ld new steps to show us our place in the un

There have only been a few times during the history of mankind when there has been such a spectacular blending of innovation in the arts, in science, and in philosophy as there was during Renaissance times.

REPLICA OF THE GUTENBERG PRESS

THE PRINTING PRESS

The invention of movable type and the mechanical printing press by Gutenberg in 1440 revolutionized reading and literacy. It represented the first time in history that books could be mass-produced. By the year 1500, printing press businesses had spread throughout Western Europe, ensuring that millions more people in the coming centuries could learn to read and write and have books of their own.

WHAT IS A RENAISSANCE MAN OR WOMAN?

If anyone ever says to you, "you're a Renaissance person," it's a huge compliment. It means that you are good at everything you do in lots of different areas. For example, Leonardo da Vinci was considered to be a Renaissance man because he was masterful in both the arts and sciences.

MONA LISA BY LEONARDO DA VINCI

A wesome! Now you know more about the legacy of the Renaissance. You can find more Renaissance books from Baby Professor by searching the website of your favorite book retailer.

Visit

BABY PROFESSOR
EDUCATION KIDS

www.BabyProfessorBooks.com

to download Free Baby Professor eBooks
and view our catalog of new and exciting
Children's Books

Manufactured by Amazon.ca
Bolton, ON